Piano / Vocal / Guitar

the very best of... STING & THE POLICE

ISBN 0-7935-9424-3

HAL•LEONARD®
CORPORATION
7777 W. Bluemound Rd. P.O. Box 13819 Milwaukee, WI 53213

Visit Hal Leonard Online at
www.halleonard.com

MESSAGE IN A BOTTLE

Written and Composed by
STING

C♯m9
3rd
Amaj7
B7
F♯m
C♯m9
3rd
Amaj7
B7
F♯m
Res - cue me be - fore I fall in - to des - pair - - o
Love can mend your life but love can break your heart
hun - dred bil - lion cast - a - ways look - ing for a home
(Con 8ve)
A
D
E
A
D
E
I'll send an S. O. S. to the world I'll send an S. O. S. to the world
loco
F♯m
D
F♯m
D
I hope that some - one gets my, I hope that some - one gets my,
F♯m
D
C♯m
A
I hope that some - one gets my mes-sage in a bot - - tle yeah.
Con 8ve
C♯m
A
To Coda
C♯m
A
mes-sage in a bot - - tle yeah.

1
F♯m
2
F♯m
Con 8ve
Con 8ve
D.𝄋. al Coda
CODA
C♯m
A
mes-sage in a bot - - tle
Con 8ve
C♯m
A
C♯m
A
mes-sage in a bot - - tle oh yeah.
F♯m
C♯m9
3rd
Amaj7
B7
F♯m
C♯m9
3rd
Amaj7
B7
loco
F♯m
C♯m9
3rd
F♯m
Repeat to fade
I'm send - ing out an S. O. S. I'm
Con 8ve

CAN'T STAND LOSING YOU

Written and Composed by
STING

C G C Asus4 B♭
not pre - pared to go on like this I can't I can't I can't stand los - ing, I
car - ry on liv - ing does - n't make no sense
I'm too full to swal - low my pride
Gm Asus4
can't I can't I can't stand los - ing, I can't I can't I can't I can't stand los - ing
1
Dm Gm Dm Gm Dm Gm Dm Gm
you I can't stand los - ing you I can't stand los -
3
f
Dm Gm Dm Gm Dm Gm Dm Gm
- ing you I can't stand los - ing you. I
3
2,𝄋 Asus4 B♭ Gm
can't stand los - ing I can't I can't I can't stand los - ing I can't I can't I

To Coda
Asus4
B♭9
can't stand los - ing I can't I can't I can't stand los - ing.
f
C9
B♭9
C9
I
Dm
guess this is our last good-bye and you don't care so I won't cry and you'll be sor - ry
p
Dm
D.S. al Coda
when I'm dead and all this guilt will be on your head I
cresc.
ff
CODA
Asus4
C
can't stand los-ing I can't I can't I
ff
Asus4
B♭
Repeat to fade
can't stand los-ing I can't I can't I can't stand los-ing I can't I can't I can't stand los-ing I

ENGLISHMAN IN NEW YORK

Written and Composed by
STING

Em A Bm A
And you can hear it in my ac - cent when I talk, I'm an
Em A Bm Em A
Eng - lish - man in New York.
You see me walk - ing down Fifth Av -
If "man-ners mak - eth man" as some -
Bm A Em A Bm A
- e - nue, a walk-ing cane here at my side.
- one said, He's the he - ro of the day.
Em A Bm A
I take it ev - 'ry - where I walk. I'm an
It takes a man to suf - fer ig - no - rance and smile. Be your - self

Em A Bm A
Eng - lish - man in New York.
no mat - ter what they say.
Woh.
Em A Bm A
I'm an a - li - en. I'm a le - gal a - li - en. I'm an
Em A Bm Em A
Eng - lish - man in New York. Woh. I'm an a - li - en.
Bm Em A 1 Bm A
I'm a le - gal a - li - en. I'm an Eng - lish - man in New York.

2
Bm
A/C♯
D
A
Mod - es - ty, pro - pri - e - ty can lead to no - to - ri - e - ty, but
Bm
F♯
you could end up as the on - ly one.
G
A
Gen - tle - ness, so - bri - e - ty are rare in this so - ci - e - ty. At
F♯/A♯
Bm
night a can - dle's bright - er than the sun.

Em9 A Bm Em9 A
Instrumental ad lib.
Bm Bm no chord
Play 4 times
drum beat
ff
Em A Bm A Em A
Takes more than com - bat gear to make a man.
Takes more than a li - cense for a
mf
Bm A Em A Bm A
gun.
Con - front your en - e - mies, a - void them when you can.
A

Em A Bm A
gen - tle - man will walk but nev - er run.
Em A Bm
If "man-ners mak - eth man" as some - one said,
Em A Bm Em A
he's the he - ro of the day. It takes a man to suf - fer ig -
Bm A Em A Bm A
- nor-ance and smile. Be your - self no mat-ter what they say. Be your - self

Em
A
Bm
A
no mat - ter what they say.
Be your - self
Em
A
Bm
Woh.
no mat - ter what they say.
Be your - self
Em
A
Bm
A
I'm an a - li - en.
I'm a le - gal a - li - en,
I'm an
no mat - ter what they say.
Be your - self
Em
A
Bm
Repeat ad lib. and Fade
En - glish - man in New York.
Woh.
no mat - ter what they say.
Be your - self

EVERY BREATH YOU TAKE

Written and Composed by
STING

Dsus
Em
D7sus
G
I'll be watch-ing you.
Ev - 'ry sin - gle day
Em
ev - 'ry word you say,
ev - 'ry game you play
C
D
Dsus
G
ev - 'ry night you stay;
I'll be watch-ing you.
C
C/B♭
Am7
G
Oh, can't you see
you be - long to me.

A7
How my poor heart aches
with ev - 'ry step you
D
D7sus
G
take.
Ev - 'ry move you make
Ev - 'ry vow you
Em
C
break,
ev - 'ry smile you fake
ev - 'ry claim you stake,
D
Dsus
Em
To Coda
I'll be watch - ing you.

Eb
F
Since you've gone I been lost with - out a trace,
I dream at night I can on -
Eb
-ly see your face.
I look a - round but it's you I can't re - place,
F
Eb
I feel so cold and I long for your em - brace.
I keep cry - ing bab-
G
Em
-y bab - y please.

C
D
Em
G
D.S. al Coda
CODA
Em
C
Oh can't you
Ev - 'ry move you make Ev - 'ry step you take,
D
Dsus
Em
I'll be watch - ing you.
D7sus
G
I'll be watch - ing you.

WALKING ON THE MOON

Written and Composed by
STING

Dm7(add G)
Dm7
B♭/C
C
we could live to - geth - er walk - ing on walk - ing on the moon
feet don't hard - ly make no sound walk - ing on walk - ing on the moon
1 Dm7(add G)
2,3 Dm7(add G)
Dm7
B♭
F
C
Gm
Some may say I'm wish - ing my days a - way
B♭
F
C
Gm
no way and if it's the price I pay

B♭
F
C
Gm
some say
to - mor - row's an - oth - er day
B♭
F
C
To Coda
you'll stay
I may as well play
Dm7(add G)
D.%. al Coda
CODA
Dm7(add G)
Dm7
B♭/C
C
Repeat to Fade
Keep it up
keep it up

FIELDS OF GOLD

Written and Composed by
STING

G D G/B A Bm7
jeal - ous sky as we walk in fields_ of gold.
jeal - ous sky as we lie in fields_ of gold.
3
G D
So she
See the
Bsus2 G
took her love for to gaze a - while_ up - on the fields_ of bar -
west wind move like a lov - er so___ up - on the fields_ of bar -
D Bsus2 G D
- ley. In his arms she fell as her hair came down a - mong_
- ley. Feel her bod - y rise when you kiss her mouth a - mong_
7
7

G/B
A
1 D
2 D
the fields of gold. Will you
the fields of gold.
G
D
G
I nev - er made prom - is - es light - ly and there have been
D
G
D
some that I've bro - ken, but I swear in the days still left we'll walk
G/B
A
D
G/B
A
in fields of gold. We'll walk in fields of gold.
3

D
Bsus2
G
D
Bsus2
G
D
G/B
A
D
Bsus2
Man - y years have passed since those
mem - ber me when the
G
D
sum-mer days a - mong the fields of bar - ley. See the
west wind moves up - on the fields of bar - ley. You can
3

Bsus2
G
D
G/B
A
chil - dren run as the sun goes down a - mong _ the fields _ of gold.
tell the sun in his jeal - ous sky when we walked in fields _ of gold,
1 D
2 D
G/B
A
You'll re -
when _ we walked in fields _ of gold,
D
G/B
A
D
G/D
D
when we walked in fields _ of gold.
G/D
D
G/D
D
1 G/D
D
2

EVERY LITTLE THING SHE DOES IS MAGIC

Written and Composed by
STING

G/B A/C♯ D G A D G A
—— my nerve_ as I've_ done from the start__
D G A D (N.C.)
CHORUS
A A D/C A/C D
Eve-ry lit-tle thing she does_ is ma - gic ev-ery-thing she
gliss.
A D/C A/C♯ D A D/C A/C♯ D
do just turns_ me on_ ev - en though my life be-fore_ was tra - gic now I know my
A D/C A/C♯ B♭ C/F
love for her__ goes on

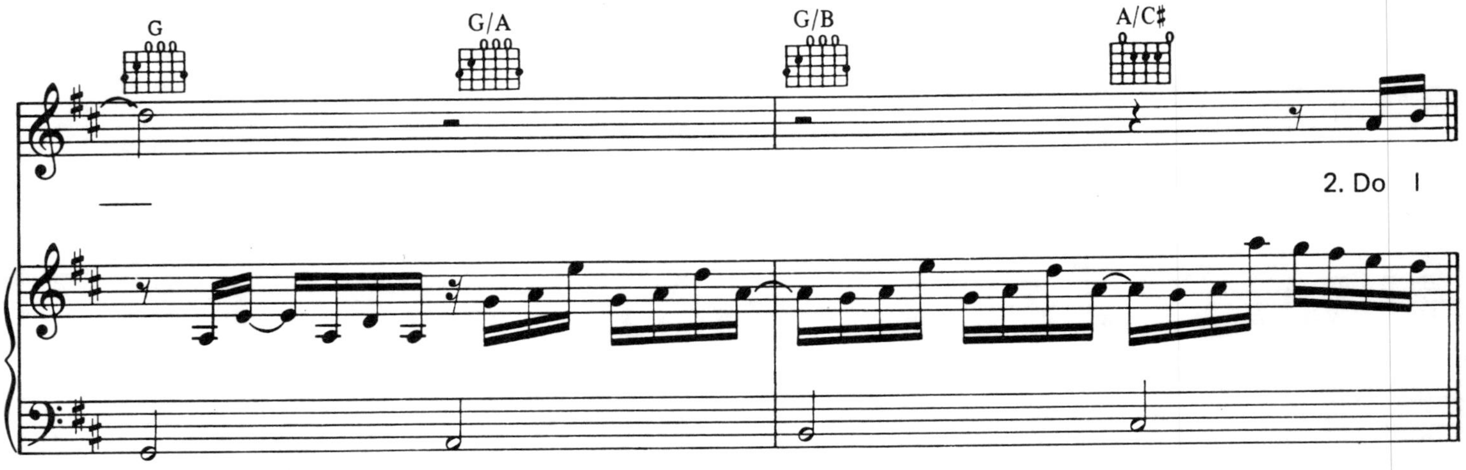

VERSE 2: Do I have to tell the story
Of a thousand rainy days since we first met
It's a big enough umbrella
But it's always me that ends up getting wet.

CHORUS: (Repeat)

Gm7 Am7 Bb Am7
and ask her if she'll mar-ry me in some old_ fash-ioned way but my
Bb C Bb C
si - lent fears have gripped_me long be-fore___ I reach_ the phone_ long be-fore_
Bb C
___ my time___ has tripped___ me must I
Bb C D G A D (N.C.) A
al - ways be a - lone (Chorus) Ev-ery lit-tle
CHORUS (Repeat)—to End

IF YOU LOVE SOMEBODY SET THEM FREE

Written and Composed by
STING

G Dm7 G F/A G
you can do the same.
some-one to des-pise.
If you want to keep
Or a pris-'ner
Dm7 G F/A G Dm7 G F/A
some-thing pre-cious,
in the dark
got to lock it up and throw a-way the key.
tied up in chains you just can't see
G Dm7 G F/A G
You want to hold on to your pos-ses-sion,
or a beast in a gild-ed cage;
don't e-ven
that's all some peo-
Dm7 G F/A G Bm7
think a-bout me.
ple ev-er want to be.
If you love some-bod-y

G
if you love some - one,
if you love
Bm7
somebod - y,
G
if you love some -
Am7
one set them free.
Dm9
G
Am7
(Free, free, set them free)
G
Set them
Dm9
G
Am7
free.
(Free, free, set them free)
G
Set them free.
Dm9
G
Am7
(Free, free, set

G
To Coda
Dm9
G
Am7
1
G
Set them free.
If it's a mir-ror
___ them free)
(Free, free, set ___ them free)
Dm7
G
2
G
Fsus
you want,
You can't con -
___ them free)
F
C/E
C
trol an in - de - pen - dent heart,
(can't love what you can't keep)
Gm7
F
C/E
Can't tear the one you love a - part.
(can't love what you

C
Gm7
F
For - ev - er con - di - tioned to be - lieve that we can't live, we can't
can't keep)
C/E
C
Gm7
live here and be hap - py with less.
With so man - y rich - es, so
F
C/E
C
man - y souls, with ev' - ry - thing we see that we want to pos - sess. If you
Dm7
G
D.S. al Coda
need some - bod - y,
CODA
Dm9
G
Am7
Repeat and Fade with vocal ad lib.
G
free.
(Free, free, set them free)
Set them

LET YOUR SOUL BE YOUR PILOT

Written and Composed by
STING

B♭
F/G
Gm
3 fr
doc - tors failed to heal you,
coun - sel leads to com - fort,
Cm7
3 fr
when no medi - cine chest
when there are no more lies
F9sus
1 F
can make you well, when no
they can tell.
2 F
Gm
3 fr
D+
No more use - less in - for -
no in - for -

Gm7
3fr
C9
E♭
3fr
ma - tion __ and the com - pass spins, the com -
ma - tion __ and the com - pass turns to no -
B♭m/D♭
C7sus
C7
- pass spins be - tween heav - en and hell.
- where, to no - where that you know well.
Let your _
B♭
B♭/A♭
G7sus
soul ______ be __ your pi - lot. _
G7
E♭
3fr
To Coda
F7sus
F7
___ Let _ your soul guide _ you, he'll guide _ you

B♭
E♭(add9)
well.
And your eyes turn towards the win -
Fsus
F
Cm7(add4)
A♭6/9
dow pane
to the lights up-on the hill.
E♭(add9)
Fsus
F
The dis - tance seems so strange to you now,
Cm7(add4)
A♭6/9
and the dark room seems so still.
Let your

B♭
F/G
Gm
3fr
pain ___ be _ my sor - row. __
cour - age be _ my mod - el, ___
Cm7
3fr
Let _ your tears be my _ tears
that _ the north you find _ will _ be
F9sus
1 F
2 F
D.S. al Coda
too. Let _ your
true. When _ there's
CODA
F7sus
F7
Gm7
3fr
let ___ your soul guide ___ you, ______

F#+
Eb
3fr
Fsus
F
let your soul guide you up - on your
Bb
way.
(Let your soul guide you a - long the way.)
(Let your soul guide you a -
Bbm7
Let your soul guide you.
long the way.)
(Let your soul guide you a -
Repeat ad lib. and Fade
Let your soul guide you.
Let your
long the way.)
(Let your soul guide you a - long the way.)

RUSSIANS

Music by SERGEI PROKOFIEV
Lyrics by STING

G7sus G E♭ G/B
So - vi - ets. Mis - ter Krush - chev said, "We will bu - ry you." I
Cm G Cm Cm/B♭
don't sub - scribe to this point of view. It'd be such an ig - nor - ant
A♭ B♭ Fm7 B♭ Cm
thing to do if the Rus - sians love their child - ren too. How
Cm Cm/B♭ A♭ B♭ Fm Gm A♭ B♭
can I save my lit - tle boy from Op - pen - heim - er's dead - ly toy? There
is no his - tor - i - cal pre - ce - dent to put the words in the mouth of the pre - si - dent? There's

Cm Cm/B♭ A♭ B♭ G/B Cm
is no mo - no - po - ly on com - mon sense on ei - ther side of the po -
no such thing as a win - na - ble war, it's a lie we don't be - lieve
G7sus G E♭ G/B
li - ti - cal fence. We share the same bi - o - lo - gy, re -
an - y - more. Mis - ter Rea - gan says, "We will pro - tect you." I
Cm G Cm Cm/B♭
gard - less of i - de - o - lo - gy. Be - lieve me when I say
don't sub - scribe to this point of view. Be - lieve me when I say
A♭ B♭ To Coda Fm Gm A♭ B♭
to you, I hope the Rus - sians love their child - ren
to you, I hope the

Cm Ab Cm/Eb Cm/F Cm Ab Cm/Eb Cm/F Cm Ab
too.
Cm/Eb Cm/F Cm Ab
1. Cm/Eb Cm/F
2. Cm/Eb Cm/F
D.S. al Coda
There
CODA
Fm7 Bb Cm Cm/Bb Ab Cm/Bb
Rus - sians love their child - ren too.
Cm/F Cm/G Ab Cm/Bb Cm Cm/Bb Ab Cm/Bb G/B Cm

G7sus G E♭ G/B Cm
We share the same bi - o - lo - gy, re - gard - less of i - de - o -
G Cm Cm/B♭ A♭ B♭ Fm Gm
lo - gy. But what might save us, me and you, is if the Rus - sians love
A♭ B♭ Cm A♭ Cm/E♭ Cm/F Cm A♭
their child - ren too.
Cm/E♭ Cm/F Cm A♭ Cm/E♭ Cm/F Cm A♭ Cm/E♭ Cm/F
Repeat and Fade

IF I EVER LOSE MY FAITH IN YOU

Written and Composed by
STING

Asus2
A
G
You could say I lost my be - lief in the ho - ly___ church.
You could say I lost my ___ faith in the peo - ple on T. V.
that did - n't go from a bless-ing to a curse.
Dsus2(sus4)
D
Dsus2(sus4)
D
Asus2
A
You could say I
You could say I lost my be -
I nev - er saw no
G
Dsus2(sus4)
D
Dsus2(sus4)
D
To Coda
lost ___ my sense of di-rect - ion.
lief ___ in our pol-i-ti - cians.
mil-i-tar-y sol-u-tion
Asus2
A
F#m7
You could say all of this and worse, but
They all seem like game show hosts to me.

Esus2
E
F#7sus
F#7
G6
if
If
I ev - er lose ___ my faith ___ in you
Asus
A
A/B
Esus2
E
F#7sus
F#7
there'd be noth - ing left ___ for me ___ to do.
G6
1 Asus
A
2 Asus
A
Asus
A
Hey, _ hey. _
G5
E5
G5
E5
G5
E5

G5 E5 F#m7 G#m7(add4)
I could be lost in - side their
Amaj9 Bsus B F#sus2 F#
lies with - out a trace, but ev - 'ry
G#7sus G#7 B/A A B/A A6
D.S. al Coda
time I close my eyes I see your face.
CODA
Asus2 A F#m7
that did-n't al-ways end up as some-thing worse, but

Esus2
E
C#m7
let me say this first:
Bsus2
B
C#7sus
C#7
D6
if I ev - er lose my faith in you, if I ev - er lose
Esus
E
Bsus2
B
C#7sus
C#7
my faith in you there'd be noth - ing left for me to do,
D6
Esus
E
Esus2
E
there'd be noth - ing left for me to do. If I ev - er lose

F#7sus F#7 G6 Asus A A/B
my faith, if I ev - er lose my faith,
Esus2 E F#7sus F#7 G6
if I ev - er lose my faith, if I ev - er lose
Asus A Asus A G5 E5
my faith in you...
G5 E5 G5 E5 G5 E5
Repeat and Fade

WHEN WE DANCE

Written and Composed by
STING

Moderately (not too fast)

Eb
1
2
town, I'd change my name.
owns a bird that sings.
When_ he
When_ we
Bb
Eb/G
Ab
Eb
dance,
an - gels_ will run and hide_ their wings.
The priest has said my soul's_ sal - va - tion
Cm7
is in the bal - ance of_ the an - gels
and un - der - neath the wheels_

E♭
3fr
of pas - sion.
I keep the faith in my
B♭
fash - ion.
When we dance,
(I will love you more than life
E♭/G
3fr
A♭(add9)
3fr
Fm7
an - gels will run and hide their wings.
if you'll on - ly be my wife.
I'm gon-na love you night and day.
D♭
B♭
When we dance,
I'm gon-na try in ev - 'ry way.
I'm gon-na find a place to live,

Eb/G
Ab
Eb
an - gels will run and hide their wings.
give you all I've got to give. I will love you more than life
Cm7
Absus2
Fsus
F
if you'll on - ly be my wife.) If I could break down these walls
Csus
C
Fsus
F
and shout my name at heav-en's gate, I'd take these hands and I'd de-stroy the
Csus
C
Fsus
F
dark ma-chin-er-ies of fate. Ca-the-drals are bro - ken,

Absus
Ab
4fr
Absus
Ab
4fr
heav-en's no longer a - bove, and hell - fire's a prom-ise a-way I'd still be saying I'm
Eb
3fr
Cm7
3fr
Eb/Ab
3fr
Eb
3fr
still in love.
Cm7
3fr
F
He won't love you, like I
live with me. We'll have
Dm7
love you. He won't care for you this way.
chil-dren of our own. I would love you more than life

F
1
He'll _ mis - treat you if you stay. _
if _ you'll come and be my wife. _
Come _ and
2
C
F/A
B♭
When _ we dance, an - gels _ will run and hide _ their
Gm7
3 fr
1,2
E♭sus2
3
wings.
When _ we
When _ we
F
Dm7
F/B♭
dance. _
(I'm gon - na love you night and day. I'm gon - na try in ev - 'ry way.

F
Dm7
F/B♭
I'm gon-na find a place to live, give you all I've got to give.
F
Dm7
F/B♭
I will love you more than life if you'll on - ly be my wife.
F
Dm7
F/B♭
I'm gon-na love you night and day. I'm gon-na try in ev - 'ry way.)
Repeat and Fade
F
Dm7
C7sus
F
Dm7
C7sus

DON'T STAND SO CLOSE TO ME

Written and Composed by
STING

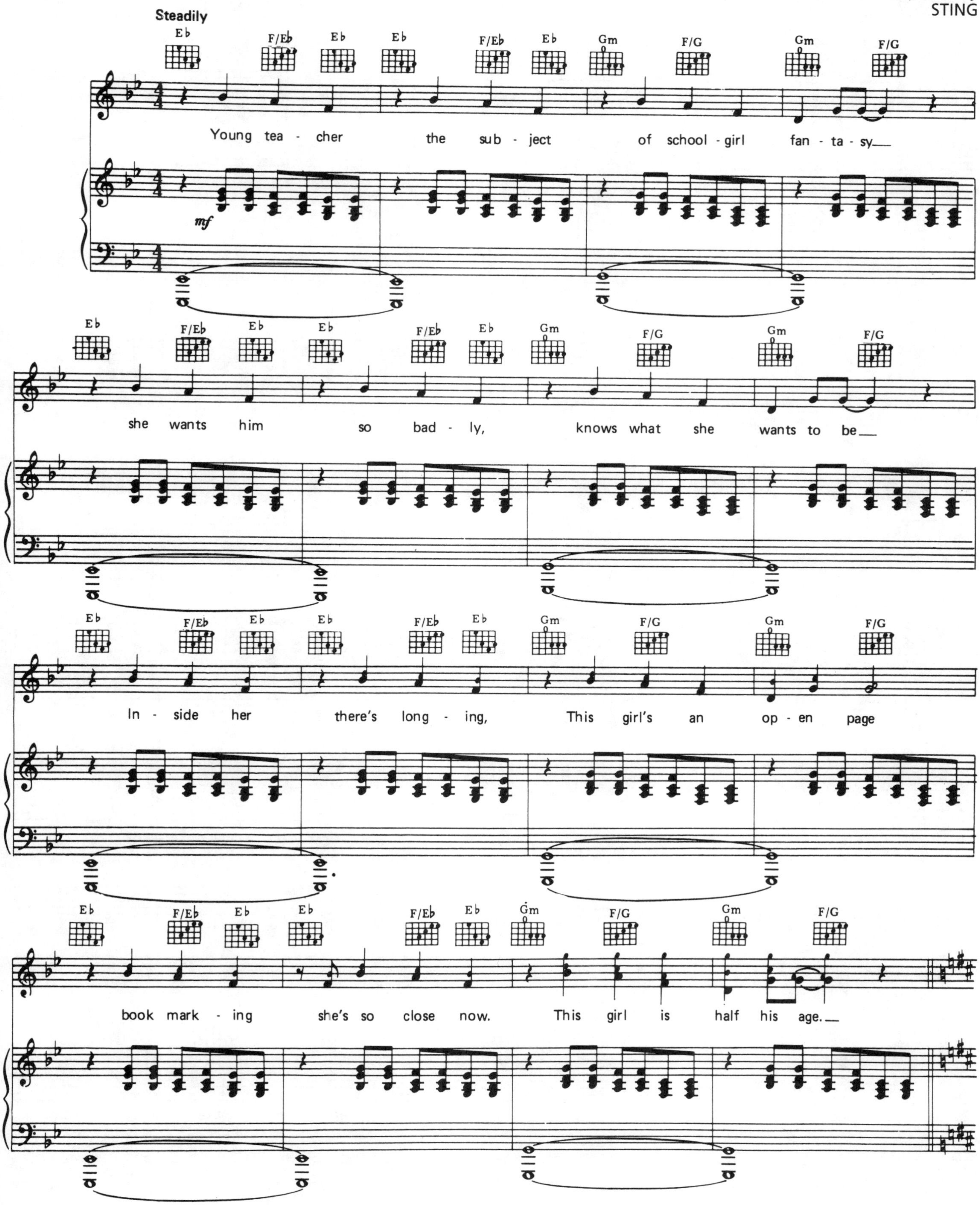

D A D A Bm A D7/A Em/A D A
Don't stand don't stand so don't stand so close to me— don't stand
D A Bm A D7/A Em/A D7/A Em/A
don't stand so don't stand so close to me.—
Eb F/Eb Eb Eb F/Eb Eb Gm F/G Gm F/G
Her friends are— so jealous you know how bad girls— get—
Loose talk— in— the class-room to hurt they try and— try—
𝄋 = Instrumental
Eb F/Eb Eb Eb F/Eb Eb Gm F/G Gm F/G
Some-times it's not so ea-sy to be the tea-cher's— pet.—
Strong words in the staff room the ac-cu-sa-tions— fly,—
Eb F/Eb Eb Eb F/Eb Eb Gm F/G Gm F/G
Temp-ta-tion frus-tra-tion so bad it makes him— cry—
it's no use he sees her he starts to shake and— cough—

Eb F/Eb Eb Eb F/Eb Eb Gm F/G Gm F/G
To Coda
wet bus stop she's wait - ing his car is warm and dry,
just like the old man in that book by Nab - a - kov.
CHORUS
D A D A Bm A D7/A Em/A
Don't stand don't stand so don't stand so close to me.
D A D A Bm A D7/A Em/A
don't stand don't stand so don't stand so close to me.
1 D7/A Em/A
2 D7/A Em/A D7/A Em/A D7/A Em/A
D.S. al Coda
CODA
D A D A Bm A D7/A Em/A
Don't stand don't stand so don't stand so close to me.
(Please don't stand so close to me)
Repeat to Fade

ROXANNE

Written and Composed by
STING

Gsus4
Cm
Fsus4
Gsus4
put on the red light
Roxanne
you don't have to put on the red light
G7sus4
To Coda
Cm
Bb
Eb
F
F
Gm
Roxanne
(put on the red light)
Roxanne
(put on the red light)
Roxanne
F/C
Bb
F/C
Eb
F
Gsus4
(put on the red light)
Roxanne
(put on the red light)
Roxanne
(put on the red light)
Oh
D.S. al Coda
CODA
Gm
Gm/F
Gm
Gm/F
Bb
I
(-anne)
(put on the red light)
Repeat to fade
Eb
F
F
Gm
F/C
Bb
Roxanne
(put on the red light)
Roxanne
(put on the red light)
Roxanne

ROXANNE '97-
PUFF DADDY REMIX

Written and Composed by
STING

G9
1
G13
2
Rules of the game, she plays the politics.
Never get through like the call is blocked.
Red light special, red light district.
Sung: Rox -
Twisted-minded like Bob's dred-locks.
E♭maj7
D7♯5
Gm9
C13
anne, you don't have to put on the red light.
Those days are o - ver, you don't have to sell your bod - y to the
night. Rox - anne, you don't have to wear that dress to - night,

C13
2fr
E♭maj7
3fr
D7♯5
walk the streets for mon - ey. You don't
Gm9
C13
2fr
E♭maj7
3fr
care if it's wrong or if it's right. Rox - anne,
D7♯5
Gm9
C13
2fr
you don't have to put on the red light. Rox -
E♭maj7
3fr
D7♯5
Gm9
- anne, you don't have to put on the red
light,
light.

C13
Ebmaj7
D7#5
you don't have to
put on the red light,
Gm9
C13
Ebmaj7
D7#5
put on the red light,
put on the red light,
To Coda
Gm9
C13
Ebmaj7
D7#5
put on the red light,
put on the red light,
oh.
Rap 3: Yo, what's the
G9
G13
hack? Dancing for the green paperback,
sitting at the bar drinkin' up cognac. But she
Rap 4: mance in the street. She's the pippist paradise.
Jewels around her leg, getting' stoned with the ice. She said, "I

G9
G13
G9
steps in the room, don't know how to act. Sweet in multi-simila to simalac. Yo, what's the hatch, catch? Wanna be around, shine.
heard of the crew, I'm the number one fan. Love the refugees down from the islands." Drop in the Bentleys with her pretty, pretty friends,
G13
G9
She wants to party, have a good time.
sippin' colada. Everyday is a weekend.
She feels kinda heartly, feelin', feelin' fine.
Heard your name was Pras out of Brooklyn and
1
2
N.C.
G13
Dig it on her life just to get a goldmine. Ro-
fifty million plays was your total SoundScan.
I
E♭maj7
D7♯5
Gm9
C13
loved you since I knew you,
I would-n't talk down to you.
I

Ebmaj7
D7#5
Gm9
N.C.
have to tell you just how I feel. I won't share you with an-oth-er boy.
Ebmaj7
I know my mind is made up
D7#5
Gm9
so, put a-way your make-up.
C13
Ebmaj7
Told you once, I won't

D7#5
Gm9
tell you a - gain, it's a bad way.
C13
D.S. al Coda
Rox -
CODA
Gm7
N.C.
Put on the red light.
Rox - anne, Rox - anne,
G9
G13
I wan - na be your man.
Gm7
N.C.
Put on the red light.
Rox - anne, Rox - anne,
1
G9
G13
I wan - na be your man.
2
G9
N.C.
I wan - na be your man.